Loving Me Within the Foster Care Walls

Written by Katina Boykin

Illustrated by Brittany Deanes

Copyright © 2022 by Katina Boykin

Illustrated by Brittany Deanes

All rights reserved. No part of this publication may be reproduced, distributed, or transmitted in any form or by any means, including photocopying, recording, or other electronic or mechanical methods, without the prior written permission of the publisher, except in the case of brief quotations embodied in critical reviews and certain other noncommercial uses permitted by copyright law.

Paperback ISBN: 978-1-951300-60-9

Liberation's Publishing ~ West Point, MS.

Loving Me Within the Foster Care Walls

Love endures with patience and serenity, love is kind and thoughtful, and is not jealous or envious; love does not brag and is not proud or arrogant. It is not provoked (nor overly sensitive and easily angered); it does not take into account a wrong endured. It does not rejoice at injustice' but rejoice in truth (when right and truth prevail). Love bears all things (regardless of what comes), believe all things (looking for the best in each one), hopes all things (remaining steadfast during difficult times) endures all things (without weakening). Love never fails (it never fades nor ends). 1 Corinthians 13:4-8 (Holy Bible, Amplified)

In Loving Me Within the Foster Care Walls, a worker within the Foster Care Walls steps in and takes the foster child on a journey to show him what love is. She made the choice to love him and help tear down the walls he built up from being in the system. Through this inspiring book, it will show what unconditional love looks like, and how it saves one child's life through loving him and never giving up on him.

Unconditional love isn't temporary; it's a lifetime commitment!

-A Foster Mother who loves unconditionally-

Sincerely,

Acknowledgement

First and foremost, I would like to Thank God. Without him, I would be nothing. I would like to acknowledge Corry Boykin (husband), Shaniah Dancy (Daughter), and Caeson Dancy (Son). I push myself to be the best for you all! I am very thankful to Liberation Publishing, Nicole Mangum and Brittany Deanes for this opportunity.

Dedication

I would like to dedicate this book to Shaniah and Caeson Dancy. You two are my world! To Shirley Shumpert (granny), Nancy Westmoreland (granny), and Jerry Westmoreland (daddy); I miss ya'll so much! I wish you all were here to witness another sweet moment in my life. Although you are not here physically, I know you're here spiritually.

Aiden was seven years old when he entered foster care. Before this, he never knew what love felt like. He was so sad. Foster care is where he met Maria. Maria was the first person to show him love. They became friends.

Maria took care of foster children before. She has been a caregiver for two years; she has seen many children come in and out of foster care. She immediately fell in love with Aiden. She could tell he was a sweet-kind young boy.

It took Aiden time to process someone caring for him and loving him. He wanted to ask her a question. "Miss Maria, he asked, "Can I ask you a question?"

"Yes Aiden." She replied looking him in the eyes. "You can ask me whatever you want." "What is the definition of love? I'm asking because when the school found out that my mother was homeless, they took me away from her. They said that was love, but it doesn't feel like love to me."

"I understand Aiden." Maria stated. "It is hard to be without your mom. I know she misses you as much as you miss her. You will be safe here with us. We will take good care of you for her.

"Let's go outside and have a seat on the steps." Maria walked Aiden outside, and they took a seat on the steps. "Love is a connection. It is a bond that people share with each other. For instance, when a child is loved; you are protected, you are clothed, fed, and you are guided

"Love is what parents show to their children. It is what a husband and wife show to each other. It is having quality time together, giving gifts, communicating needs and wants. Showing love to a child is the start of a happy life for them. Aiden, can I ask you a question?" She stated. "Do you think we show you love here?

Yes! Aiden explained. "Yes, you do show love. I think so! You are so nice!" Maria smiled. "Just because a child is in foster care, does not mean they do not have love. It takes a special person to love a child and to treat them right. You are loved! We will continue to show you love while you're here."

It takes longer to bond with a foster child. They have usually gone through some pretty hard situations. They may not be trusting of others first off. Most foster children have some type of mental health issues, because of the household living arrangements. ADD, ADHD, depression, anxiety and conduct behavior are just a few.

This could all be prevented if parents would take the time to show love and affection to the needs of the child. When shown love to a child and they grow older, they're able to show love when they become an adult. "Miss. Maria," Aiden asked. "What does mental health issues mean?" "I will be glad to explain that to you." Maria replied.

Let's start with attention deficit disorder or ADD. This disorder is caused by behavior problems such as not following directions, not keeping up with assignments, or having problems being around people. Attention Deficit Hyperactivity or ADHD is a behavioral condition that causes problems focusing on daily activities, getting organized or thinking before acting.

Depression is very serious and more common. This affects how one feels, thinks, or acts. Anxiety has to do with your emotions, your thought process, and your physical changes. When you worry a lot, your emotions and thought process are all over the place.

Conduct problem is a mental disorder. It is usually diagnosed when you are a child.

Always remember this Aiden; having a place to go is HOME, having a person to LOVE is family, and to have them both is a BLESSING!

The End!

www.ingramcontent.com/pod-product-compliance
Lightning Source LLC
Chambersburg PA
CBHW042036120526
44592CB00028B/74